A New True Book

HELICOPTERS

By David Petersen

This "true book" was prepared
under the direction of
Illa Podendorf,
formerly with the Laboratory School,
University of Chicago

CHILDRENS PRESS ™

CHICAGO

PHOTO CREDITS

David Petersen—11, 12 (left), 14, 16, (2 photos), 19, 20, 22, 24 (2 photos), 26 (2 photos), 29, 31, 38, 41

Bell Helicopter (Textron)—2, 18 (left)

Historical Pictures Service—4 (2 photos)

Sikorsky Aircraft—7

Hughes Helicopters, Inc.—9 (left), 18 (right), 37, 45

Hillstrom Stock Photos—©Ray Hillstrom: 9 (right), 12 (right), 43; ©David Arndt: Cover, 28, 39

Hiller Aviation—21, 36, 44

Tony Freeman—32, 35

Bill Thomas, 34

Library of Congress Cataloging in Publication Data

Petersen, David.
  Helicopters.

  (A New true book)
  Includes index.
  Summary: Highlights basic information about the history of helicopters, their parts and how they function, and the types and uses of whirlybirds.
  1. Helicopters—Juvenile literature.
[1. Helicopters] I. Title.
TL716.P4 1983   629.133′352   82-23502
ISBN 0-516-01680-6   AACR2

TABLE OF CONTENTS

Right: Leonardo da Vinci (1452-1519) drew this flying machine. He called it an aerial screw.
Below: In 1901 Martinez Diaz designed this flying machine with turning wings.

THE HISTORY OF HELICOPTERS

The Chinese made toy helicopters as long ago as a thousand years. Five hundred years later Leonardo da Vinci, an Italian inventor, scientist, and artist, drew a flying machine that had turning wings.

In 1937, a German inventor, Henrich Focke, designed and flew a helicopter. It stayed in the air for about an hour.

Though this was the first helicopter to fly, another man invented the first workable design in 1940. He was a Russian named Igor Sikorsky.

Igor Sikorsky at the controls of the helicopter he designed.
The company he started is still designing and building helicopters.

Now there are many
different kinds of helicopters.
Each is built to do a
different job.

HELICOPTER NICKNAMES

The word "helicopter" comes from two Greek words: *helix,* which means spiral or turn; and *pteron,* which means wing. So, "helicopter" actually means "turning wings."

The helicopter has many nicknames.

Many people call helicopters whirlybirds because the wings move, or turn around.

The nickname "whirlybird" comes from the way the large blades of the helicopter turn around.

"Chopper" comes from the *chop, chop* sound some helicopters make. You can often hear a helicopter long before you can see it.

Both "flying windmill" and "flying eggbeater" come from the helicopter's strange whirling blades.

Many people call helicopters either "helos" or "copters."

The Hughes 500D has a jet-turbine engine.

HOW A HELICOPTER
FLIES

A helicopter can fly straight up and down. It does not need a runway to take off or land.

Above: This helicopter has roter blades
on top and a tail rotor.
Right: This one has rotors at each end of
its body.

The wings of a
helicopter are called rotor
blades because they rotate
or go around. The rotors
are like airplane wings.
The spinning rotors speed
through the air. This
movement creates lift so
the helicopter can take off.

FLIGHT CONTROLS

The pilot uses a lever to change the angle or "pitch" of the rotor blades. Pulling the lever up will make the chopper go up. Pushing it down will make the helo go down.

On the end of this lever is a throttle control grip. The pilot uses this to change the speed of the engine.

Engine speed is important. The more pitch, or angle, the rotor blades have, the more engine power is needed to keep them turning at the proper speed.

Close-up of flight controls

So when the pilot pulls
the lever up to make the
helo go up, he must also
twist the throttle grip to
increase engine power.
And when the pilot makes
the helo go down, he must
twist the throttle at the
same time to slow down
the engine. The pilot uses
his left hand to operate
this control.

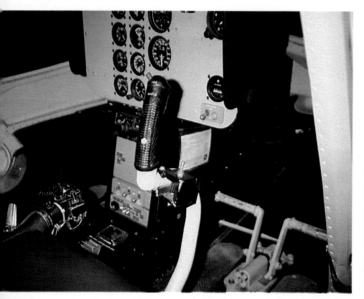

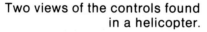
Two views of the controls found
in a helicopter.

A second control, called
the "joy stick," is mounted
on the floor in front of the
pilot's seat. The pilot
controls the joy stick with
his right hand. It makes

16

the chopper move forward, backward, or sideways.

The helo will fly in the direction the joy stick is pushed. When the stick is pushed forward, the helo tilts forward. When the chopper tilts forward, the power of the rotors will pull it forward as well as hold it up. The more the rotors are tipped forward, the faster the helicopter will fly.

To fly backward, the pilot pulls the stick back. To fly to the left, he pushes the stick to the left.

When the helo stands still in the air, it is called hovering. To hover, the pilot holds the joy stick completely still and centered.

Close-up of rudder
pedals under the
hand controls.

These pedals are called
rudders. If the pilot wants
to make his helicopter turn
in a circle, he uses the
rudders. Pushing the right
pedal will make the
chopper turn to the right.
The left rudder causes the
helo to turn to the left. The
pilot controls the rudders
with his feet.

Tail rotors are controlled by rudder pedals.

These small blades are called the tail rotors. They are connected to the rudder pedals. When the pedals are pushed, the tail rotor blades move the helo to the left or right.

ENGINES

All helicopters are powered by engines. Some helicopters burn gasoline. They have an engine similar to cars.

This Hiller helicopter burns gasoline.

This helicopter has a jet engine.

Other choppers have
engines similar to jet
planes. A jet-turbine
engine doesn't burn
gasoline. Instead, it burns
a special jet fuel. This fuel
is a high grade of kerosene.
These jet choppers are
more powerful and safer.

LANDING GEAR

Helicopters can land almost anywhere. The part of a helicopter that rests on the ground is called the landing gear.

On most choppers, the landing gear is either wheels or metal tubes called skids.

Choppers with skids cannot move, or taxi, on the ground.

On most helicopters the landing gear is either wheels (left) or skids (above).

Some choppers' skids have snowshoes. They keep the skids from sinking down into the snow.

To land on water some helicopters have pontoons. These keep the choppers afloat.

FLIGHT INSTRUMENTS

The number of instruments on a chopper depends on the size of the helicopter and the job it is designed to do. All helicopters have an air-speed indicator (speedometer), altimeter (gives height above sea level), and engine gauges.

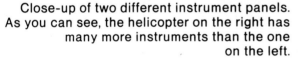

Close-up of two different instrument panels.
As you can see, the helicopter on the right has
many more instruments than the one
on the left.

The engine gauges tell
the pilot how fast the
engine is running, whether
it is running hot or cold,
and if the oil has enough
pressure.

FLIGHT HELMETS

The pilot's helmet has a built-in microphone and two radio earphones. The pilot can talk to other aircraft and to the people in airport control towers.

A flight helmet usually has two face shields. One is clear, for flying at night. The other face shield is dark, for flying in the bright sunlight.

The helmets have
"earmuffs" in them. They
protect the pilots' ears
from the loud noises made
by the chopper's engines
and rotors.

Most military pilots wear
helmets. Other pilots just
wear earphones.

LOOKING AT HELICOPTERS

Alouette

The Alouette is one of
the most popular
whirlybirds made.

The Alouette has one
large jet-turbine engine. It
flies as high as 20,000 feet.
It can lift 1,308 pounds,
or carry seven passengers.

CARGO HELICOPTERS

This large, double-rotored whirlybird is a cargo helicopter.

Cargo helicopters can carry people, supplies, and equipment. As many as twenty-five people can ride in one of these choppers at the same time. It can carry a couple of jeeps, a cannon, or a thousand-gallon water trailer.

With two sets of rotors this cargo helicopter does not need a tail rotor.

A large metal hook is attached to the bottom of many helicopters. The hook can be opened and closed by the pilot.

A long steel cable is attached to the hook. On the other end of the cable is another hook. All sorts of things can be carried by a helicopter.

Carrying things on the end of a cable is called sling loading.

Helicopters are often
used for observation flights.
In an observation flight, the
pilot will take someone,
the "observer," up so he or
she can look over a large
area of land or ocean from
the air.

OTHER HELICOPTERS

Small helicopters are often used to train new pilots. After a new pilot has learned to fly a small one, he will learn to fly some of the larger ones.

Choppers are used for observation flights, police patrolling of highways, pilot training, crop dusting (spraying and seeding farm crops), and carrying passengers.

Some helicopters can carry stretchers.

    Many people use
helicopters. They take
accident victims to
hospitals, carry passengers
into and out of places with
no roads, and pick up and
deliver large objects.

Only the military is interested in camouflaging its helicopters.

This helicopter has been camouflaged. It has been painted so it will blend into the background and be hard to see.

Many companies paint their choppers bright, pretty colors. Sometimes the name of the company is painted on the chopper, too.

SAFETY INSPECTION

Each time a helicopter is to be flown, the crew checks it. They look for such things as loose nuts and bolts and oil or gas leaks.

This inspection is called the preflight. The preflight inspection will be done three times: once by the pilot, once by the copilot, and once by the mechanic in charge of the helo.

All these men will be riding in the chopper, and they know that their safety—and the safety of their passengers—depends on how well their whirlybird is inspected before takeoff.

A postflight inspection is done as soon as the helicopter lands. The pilot will write a report telling how well the copter flew. Strange noises, vibrations, and anything else that might indicate future problems are reported.

This report is kept in a logbook. A logbook is a record of the helicopter's history. By looking at the logbook, a pilot or mechanic who is not familiar with the helicopter can tell everything about it. They know what problems it has had in the past and how long it has been since different engine parts were rebuilt.

Safety inspections are
important. All good pilots
take these inspections
seriously ... wouldn't *you*?

HELICOPTERS TODAY

Helicopters are very important. They can do jobs that no other vehicles—airplanes, trucks, or ships—can do. That's because choppers can

take off and land straight
up and down, and also
stand still in the air.

Engineers are now
building stronger and faster
helicopters to do even
bigger jobs.

WORDS YOU SHOULD KNOW

altimeter(al • TIM • ih • ter)—an instrument in an aircraft that measures how high it is

cable(KAY • bil)—a thick, strong rope made of twisted wire

camouflage(KAM • ih • flahj)—a way of hiding people or things with colors or patterns that make them look like their surroundings

gauge(GAYJ)—a measuring instrument

hover(HUV • er)—to stay in one place in the air

logbook(LOG • book)—a record of a ship or aircraft

pitch(PITCH)—slope, slant, or angle

pontoon(pon • TOON)—a structure used in place of wheels so aircraft can land on water

rotor(ROH • ter)—the wings of a helicopter

rudders(RUHD • erz)—the pedals in a helicopter that make the machine turn

skids(SKIHDZ)—metal tubes used as landing gear on a helicopter

spiral(SPY • rul)—to turn

throttle(THROT • il)—a lever that controls the speed of a helicopter

vibration(vye • BRAY • shun)—very rapid movement back and forth

INDEX

About the Author

David Petersen is a freelance writer living in Durango, Colorado. Before going freelance, David spent several years as managing editor of a small magazine based in California. He has had over 100 articles published in a variety of magazines and newspapers throughout the country.

In addition to his professional writing and editing, David teaches writing at Fort Lewis College in Durango. He holds a B.A. in Social Sciences from Chapman College in Orange, California and a B.A. in Creative Writing from Fort Lewis.